God

Jewish Choices for Struggling with the Ultimate

Edited by Josh Barkin

Torah Aura Productions

D1366590

ISBN 10: 1-934527-08-4

ISBN 13: 978-1-934527-08-5

Copyright © 2008 Torah Aura Productions

Published by Torah Aura Productions. All rights reserved.

Torah Aura Productions • 4423 Fruitland Avenue, Los Angeles, CA 90058

(800) BE-Torah • (800) 238-6724 • (323) 585-7312 • fax (323) 585-0327

E-MAIL <misrad@torahaura.com> • Visit the Torah Aura website at www.torahaura.com

MANUFACTURED IN THE UNITED STATES

This book is for Sara, who daily teaches me the meaning of *ezer k'negdo*.

And for Jane, Joel, and Alan, who are very, very patient.

—JB, November, 2007

The editor, the publisher, and the contributing authors dedicate this project in memory of Joel Shickman, whose music, menschlekhite, and words of Torah continue to inspire us all.

Contents

Foreword

When I was in college, I took a class called "The Problem of God in Comparative Perspective." We looked at various philosophical questions about God, and the different ways that different religions solved them.

"The Problem of God in Comparative Perspective" was a funny name for a class. I'd thought that I was the only one who had problems with God. It turned out that pretty much everyone else had problems, too.

One day, we were having a really complex discussion about some tough abstract ideas. Things were getting confusing and emotional. The professor, who had been standing at the board, suddenly sat down. Then he took his set of board markers and gave one to everyone in the class.

"Take a section of the board for yourself," he said, "and diagram your thoughts. Ready, set, go."

So we all stood up there and drew silly pictures and circles and graphs and lines all over the place. Then we each got to play teacher, explaining our thoughts to everyone else, pointing at the board and scribbling notes everywhere.

It was the best theological discussion I've ever had. As a Jewish teacher, I've been trying ever since to replicate that day in Dr. Smith's class. This book is an attempt. It's written by a bunch of authors. We gave them all markers and let them write on the board. We're also giving you a marker.

Take a section of the board for yourself and diagram your thoughts. Ready, set, go.

It's important for me to thank my teachers Brian Smith, Joel Grishaver, Rachel Adler, Paul Kipnes, Michael Zeldin, Isa Aron, and Sara Lee for showing me how to appreciate the joy and fulfillment that comes from thinking carefully (and in an educative way) about God. My grandmother, Trudy Lesem, continues to teach me to be a critical person who questions everything, and my parents, Caryn and Steve Barkin, taught me the importance of arguing with love. My fiancé, Sara Mason, teaches me everything.

How This Book Works

Start with this premise: Judaism offers at least two (and usually many more) answers to every question.

We collected thirteen questions about God. Then we found a bunch of rabbinical students, young Jewish teachers, and other new voices in the Jewish world. We asked them the questions, and they gave us their answers. Sometimes they agreed. Sometimes they didn't. Some of their answers are really traditional. Some of them are off-the-wall. All of their answers are Jewish answers to Jewish questions.

What you're holding in your hands is mostly a collection of their best work.

Each of the thirteen questions is a chapter in this book. Each chapter begins with a scenario or a problem that sets up the big question. Then you get to read the three or four best answers from our authors. (You can learn more about the authors in the section at the end of the book.) Last, there's some sort of task that asks you to reflect on what you've read and figure out what you think and feel about it.

A Word About Words

The words we use to talk about God have always been important to Jewish teachers and learners.

A *sofer*—a person who writes a Torah scroll—is instructed to take extra-special care when writing seven names of God: *El, Elohim, Adonai, YHWH, Ehyeh-Asher-Ehyeh, Shaddai,* and *Tz'vaot* (*Avot d'Rabbi Natan* 34). In the Talmud, our rabbis teach that another of God's names is

Shalom, and they suggest that we should not greet each other using the word *Shalom* in an unholy place (Shabbat 10b). According to the Kabbalistic tradition, God took the letters of God's name, jumbled them up, and made the world out of them (*Sefer Yetzirah* 9). When we're talking about God, names and words are powerful and important.

You may know that Hebrew is a gendered language. That means that all words, even for inanimate objects like tables and forks, are assigned a gender. That doesn't mean that we think tables or forks are male or female. It just means that the Hebrew language uses male verbs and adjectives when discussing a "male" object and female verbs and adjectives in the case of a "female" object.

This becomes a problem with God. Though Jewish texts sometimes talk about God using male or female language and metaphor, Judaism understands God as being neither male nor female (or maybe *both* male and female and everything in between). But because Hebrew is a gendered language, people translating Hebrew into English often use words like "He" or "She" when referring to God.

In this book we've made the decision to avoid gendered English language whenever possible. We think this is truest to the Jewish idea that God is without gender (or God is "beyond" gender).

But there's a big exception. This is a book written by lots of authors, all of whom have their own ideas, feelings, and beliefs when it comes to God language. So when possible, we've allowed the authors to use their own choices when they refer to God. For that reason, sometimes you'll see pieces written by someone trying to avoid gendered language, and sometimes you'll find authors using words like "Him" or "It" or "Her" or "His," while other times authors prefer to use Hebrew words like *Adonai* or *Elohim*.

These are all legitimate ways to talk about God, and we encourage you—when you talk about God—to use the words that make you most comfortable.

Chapter 1
God?

You've probably heard of Hannah Szenes. She was a Hungarian Jew who moved to *Eretz Yisrael* just before the Holocaust started. She was eighteen. While in Israel she joined the British army and trained to be a paratrooper. She also began writing poetry in Hebrew.

Hannah Szenes was not religious. She didn't go to synagogue, and she was by all accounts uninterested in the rituals, commandments, and customs of Judaism. But she wrote this poem:

My God, My God, I pray that these things never end,
The sand and the sea,
The rush of the waters,
The crash of the Heavens,
The prayer of humanity.

Examine Szenes' poem carefully. As you do, think about the following questions. You may want to note your initial answers.

1. Why would someone who was not religious write a poem about God?

2. Can you be an atheist or an agnostic and still be a Jew?

3. Is it possible to believe in God if you can't prove God exists?

4. In 1944, Hannah Szenes parachuted into Yugoslavia. Soon after she was captured by the Nazis and thrown into prison. Before she was executed she was brutally tortured. While in prison, do you think she believed in God?

We asked, *"Is there a God?"*

Ari

Infinitely, yes. That's my simple answer to this difficult question, though the path that led me to this answer was a bit more complicated.

By nature I am a scientist—logic is the source of my belief and the way that I accept truth. If I cannot explain something logically, then I'm not willing to believe it. In order to accept the idea of God, I needed to find a logical way of explaining God that worked for me. And my answer came from the realm of math and science.

When I was in college, studying various scientists and their discoveries, I recognized that a great number of the thinkers who brought us the greatest advances throughout history were also deeply religious thinkers—Descartes, Newton, Einstein. Their struggles to understand our universe went hand-in-hand with their struggles to find and understand God. The further they pushed in seeking truth, the more they found order in the universe. Logically, there must be some kind of source from which the physical laws of our universe originated.

For me, I found this source by studying the concept of infinity. Infinity describes both the immenseness of the never-ending chain of numbers and the minuscule nature of the never-ending chain of decimal places. It is not bound by time or space, and at the same time it can describe uniqueness in a way that no computer could ever do. The concept of infinity exists beyond the pale of human comprehension, and yet it is fundamental to our universe, creating nuances and vastness that provide for the needs of life. This is how we describe God, and to me this idea of infinity provided enough of a logical basis for acceptance of the concept of a God. By studying infinity I found God.

And surprisingly enough, it is the idea of infinity that gives us limits. (This is stuff you'll learn in calculus, if you end up taking it. Who knew calculus could describe God?) Judaism describes our relationship with

God in terms of limits—the commandments we are given. But we also have limits in our physical universe—the physical laws that separate what is possible from what is not. As much as the concept of infinity exists in our world and acts upon it, that is where I say there really is God.

How does Ari define God in scientific terms?

Lydia

How do you know that you love your parents? Can you see it or measure it? What about your friends? Your dog? How do you know, without a doubt, that music is important? That is has the ability to move you? How do you that something is funny? What would you do if you never had a full-out, suffocating, snort-producing belly laugh? And so, in the long-standing Jewish tradition of answering questions with questions, I would continue by asking: Is it worth it to not believe in God? In our world of science and reason it is easy to "prove empirically" that God does not exist. However, I'm inclined to believe that it just wouldn't be worth it. Rabbi Jonathan Sacks, the Chief Rabbi of England, writes, "Of course it is possible to live a life without God, just as it is possible to live a life without humor, or music, or love; and one can no more prove that God exists than one can prove these other things exist to those who lack a sense of humor, or to whom Schubert is mere noise, or love a figment of the romantic imagination."

The real issue is that it is hard, almost superhuman, to believe. We live in a world of non-believers—in the environmental issues that we face, in the Holocaust, in the power of kindness, in hope. But if we can allow ourselves to take that leap of faith, that jump into the unknown void (not unlike Indiana Jones and his walk over the invisible bridge in his search for the Holy Grail), the reward is deep and wide—like a first kiss, a song that takes you on a journey back in time, a laugh with a best friend that speaks of your shared history and memory. Rabbi Sacks knew this—he knew that one can live a life without things like humor or music or love, but it would be a smaller, more circumscribed and impoverished life. How much more so in the case of faith in God. My advice to you: don't stress over finding faith. If you want it (and you must chose to want it), faith will come as naturally as laughter or tapping your feet to a good tune. So if you are a person who wants to suck the good stuff out of life, in the legendary words of both George Michael and Limp Bizkit, "You gotta have faith, a-faith, a-faith!"

How do you think Lydia would define the word "faith"?

Shira

My first memory of God was when I was four years old. I was sitting on my front porch at dusk. Accidentally, I was locked out of the house alone. I sat on the porch knowing I should be afraid. It was then that I had my first conversation with God. I asked something to take care of me, keep me company, and it did. Everything was going to be ok – even if I lay down and spent the night on the stoop – it was me and God enjoying a starry evening outside together.

I do not remember when I stopped talking to God; probably in high school. Among my friends it was clear: Believing in God was for backwards, simple-minded people who needed to follow orders rather then make their own decisions. It was not progressive or intelligent to pray. Being Jewish was cool, but at that point it seemed mostly about latkes and lox. Davening seemed to be about history and community, not God and faith.

The more I tried to push away the notion that God was real, the more I felt sad about a random scientific explanation for the world. It wasn't enough for me; I wanted the faith that I had at four years old. I wanted it to be okay because God would be there whenever I chose to talk to her.

When I was nineteen I decided that the answer to "Is there really a God?" was unimportant. Instead I figured "Better people than I have believed in God and gotten away with it." Gandhi, Dr. Martin Luther King, Jr., Rabbi Abraham Joshua Heschel, my grandmother, Lillian Schonwald. It was not only uneducated people who relied on faith; it

14

was people I dreamt of emulating, people who have used their belief in a universal God to face fear with more hope and conviction than I could even imagine. So others may say believing in God is stupid or crazy, a terrible crutch. But crutches help your body heal when it's broken. If faith could be the support I needed to heal the part of me that felt broken, then I wanted to immediately fill my prescription. I wanted to feel as cared for as a grownup as I did at four years old. And at least I could say I was in really, really good company.

Why is belief in God important to Shira?

Sara

When I came home after my first semester of college, I announced to my father, the rabbi, "Dad, I don't believe in God anymore. I'm atheist now." He looked at me. I expected him to be angry. He wasn't. I was confused. Here I was, taking my moment as the rebellious teenager. I wanted something dramatic! Instead he said, "Don't worry. When you come back, God will be there."

I wasn't so sure. I had struggled with the patriarchal concept of God that I'd learned as a child. I had thought about God as a big man in the sky. I had even tried talking to him. I had tried squeezing my eyes shut in services and saying, "Please, God, what I really want is...fill-in-the-blank...and can you please deliver it this time?" I had tried lying in my bed and in the quiet dark asking, "Are you there, God? It's me, Sara..." with no response. Apparently, I didn't know how to talk to this kind of God, and this kind of God wasn't much for talking to me, either.

I gave up on personal prayer and instead began to struggle with the words in the *siddur*. But the Hebrew that I didn't understand brought me no closer. Finally, I gave up the struggle. That Rosh Hashanah I stood resolutely silent while the rest of the congregation sang *Avinu Malkeinu*. I was done with that Father, that King.

But about six months into my new atheism I began to feel empty, even emptier than I did when I tried to talk to a God that didn't answer. So I began to read what other people thought about God.

Eventually I stumbled over Mordecai Kaplan, and from his books I learned about God, not as a Being, but as the Process that makes the world work the way it does. I realized that just because the first way I learned about God didn't work for me, it didn't mean there is no God; I simply needed a new way to understand God. For weeks and months and years I have considered this idea further, and little by little the emptiness has filled.

God does exist, in so many forms and in so many ways for different people that sometimes it can be hard for us to decide what belief is *ours*. While we may be taught to understand God in one way, we might actually understand God better in a way that we haven't thought yet. To *keep* thinking about God and turning the question of what we believe around and around in our minds then becomes the way that we can best keep God present in our lives.

It turns out that my dad was right: When I came back, God *was* there. God had been there all along.

What do you think Sara's dad meant when he said "When you come back, God will be there"?

Does God exist?

This book is about struggling with God, and here you'll find the biggest, hardest question in the very first chapter. Before reading on (and exploring a whole bunch of other theological questions), take some time to think through this "big question." Divide the space below into three spaces. Label one space, "Stuff I Know I Believe About God." Label the second, "Stuff That I Know Isn't True About God." Label the third, "Stuff I'm Not Sure About." Then, fill in the spaces with bullet points. (You may want to use Ari, Lydia, Shira, and Sara to help you figure out what kind of stuff you can put on your chart.)

Chapter 2
Cosmogony

Aristotle was a Greek guy. He lived around 350 B.C.E. If you've heard Aristotle's name before, it's for good reason. Along with those of Plato and Socrates, Aristotle's teachings are the basis for Western philosophy. The whole idea of trying to figure out logical answers to philosophical questions comes from them.

Aristotle wrote,

> "If there has been a first man he must have been born without father or mother—which is repugnant to nature. For there could not have been a first egg to give a beginning to birds, or there should have been a first bird which gave a beginning to eggs; for a bird comes from an egg."

Basically, this is the first time someone asked, "Which came first, the chicken or the egg?"

It's a problem that's frustrating in its simplicity. The first chicken must have hatched out of an egg. But eggs don't come out of nowhere. They come from chickens. And therein, as Shakespeare would say, lies the rub.

To philosophers, this issue is called *cosmogony*. The question about the chicken and the egg is really a question about the universe.

Basic observation shows us that everything was created by something. People are created by their parents. Buildings are created by people. The sand on the beach is created by ocean tides that finely grind up rocks and minerals. We could go on and on.

If we accept (and it's okay if you don't, but play along for now) that God was the initial creator—the force that set everything in motion at the very Beginning—then we have a problem. How can God be an exception to our very basic understanding that everything was created by something else?

In other words: If God created everything, then who created God?

As you think about your own stance on the issue of cosmogony, ponder the following:

1. Why does it matter who created God?

2. In what ways is the chicken-and-the-egg a good question? In what ways is it a stupid question?

3. Why do you think people have been pondering this question for so long?

We asked, "Who created God?"

Joel S.

Wouldn't it be cool if we could say WE created God? Then WE could make up when God was to blame for the bad stuff and when WE could get credit for doing the good stuff. Or what if we could blame our rabbis and priests and imams for creating God? It would be much easier to dismiss their holy rants and antiquated commandments if we thought that they were just quoting a made-up deity who gave them better credibility.

But what if we took our often-rushed-through, sung-to-every-melody-on-earth *piyyut* (Jewish liturgical poem) *Adon Olam* at face value?

> *Adon olam, asher malakh b'terem kol y'tzir nivra.*

> Ruler of the universe, who ruled before every created-thing was created.

Is it comforting to believe that God was, is now, and forever shall be in glory, or is it troublesome?

If we accept that God is the Ultimate Creator, we might have to believe that there is a purpose for us in this world. Not so bad for us to believe when things are going our way and we feel that God intended for us to enrich the world with the gifts that God bestowed upon us. A little difficult for us to believe when we feel aimless, unmotivated, and worthless. Much more challenging for us to believe when we do hurtful things in order to get ahead.

When asked by his students, "Where is God?" the Kotzker Rebbe would reply, "Whenever we let God in." To accept that God is every-time is a good way to begin to believe that God is every-where, which can be a very comforting thought. While God can sometime seem like a Great Punisher waiting for us to make a mistake, our *paytan* (Jewish liturgical poet) of *Adon Olam* welcomed the constant presence of God.

> *V'im ruhi, g'vi'ati, Adonai li v'lo ira.*

With my spirit, my body, God is with me, I will not fear.

Perhaps it's the constant of God; perhaps it's the power of God. To believe in God as being unique and above all created things gives me strength when I'm weak and humility when I'm strong, just as it does to many of the Jews who take the words of *Adon Olam* to heart.

According to Joel S., what does it mean for God to be the "Ultimate Creator"?

Shira

Our parents have names like Susie, Kim, Alex, or Aaron, but most of us call them by titles: Mom, Mommy, Ima, Dad, or Aba. Can someone be a parent if they have never given birth, raised, or adopted a child? Your birth is what turned two people into your parents. Can someone who has never designed a building or a home call himself an architect? God also has a name, YHVH, but it was the creation of this Universe that turned God from a storyless force with an unpronounceable name into the originator of the universe, our God.

I do not believe God is an old man with a big white beard looking down on us. I believe God is beyond our comprehension and description. I think it would take more than our five senses to understand the full spectrum of any force able to instigate the creation of this amazing and diverse world, especially since our fellow organisms have senses that we don't even have (I always thought sonar would be lots of fun). The force that existed in the universe became Divine when its power was used to create. If that force had only been destructive, nothing would exist to call it a God. Like a president without a country or any citizens. It is us humans, all the animals and plants, the planets and the universe itself whose creation gave YHVH the title God. And when we use our powers to create, to nurture and sustain life and beauty, we are also acting *B'Tzelem Elohim*: in the image of God, Now who created that force that created everything?

What does the act of creation have to do with God's name?

22

Uri

I was sitting at my computer screen when a question crossed my mind. Who made this computer? The Apple company made my computer. Who made the Apple company? Mr. Steve Jobs created the Apple company. Who created Steve Jobs? I assume Mr. and Mrs. Jobs created him. [Editor's note: Actually, Steve Jobs was adopted, so he was created by Joanne Carole Schieble and Abdulfattah John Jandali. Wikipedia knows everything.] Who created them? Who created those people? And them and them and them? You see where this is going. Eventually I had asked my way back to the creation of Adam and Eve, the first humans on Earth. God created them Adam and Eve. Who created God?

I was stuck. The Bible doesn't speak of anything existing before God. I could not consult science for this answer because God may be outside the realm of science. What was I to do? I really needed an answer to this question. It bothered me so much. Steve Jobs has a creator but God doesn't? Everything needs a creator, right? Or so I thought.

God is the only entity in the universe that causes things to be created but has no cause itself. God has always existed, exists now, and will continue to exist in the future. How do I know all of this? I know because of God's name. Yup, that's right. God's name holds the answer to this ever-elusive question. Let's take a look.

God's proper name, if you will, is spelled in Hebrew Yod and Hey, Vav and Hey (YHVH. We don't know how to pronounce it anymore, so when we come across it in the *siddur* or in the Torah we say *Adonai* as a substitute]. This name and, more importantly, the letters that comprise it are very significant. The Hebrew root Hey Vav (sometimes Yod) Hey is the root of the word that translates as "to be". In *Adon Olam* we say *Vehu **Haya**, Vehu **Hoveh**, Vehu **Yihiyeh**,* God was, is, and will be. All of those words share the same root as God's name. In other words, God is everlasting, and therefore that is what we call God.

So who created God? Nobody, nothing; the question doesn't apply. God is outside of time and space and therefore needs no creator in order to exist. Names give us a lot of information about a person, place, or thing. Now on to other questions, like who created TiVo?

According to Uri, how is it that "the question doesn't apply"?

Which came first?
Chicken or egg?

The ancient Greek philosophers (Plato, Socrates, Aristotle...) used to write their philosophical opinions in the form of plays. If you pick up one of their books today, it looks like a script of a scene in which two (or three or four) people are arguing about a philosophical issue. They have their discussion, covering all the basic points of the philosophical issue at hand, and then someone wins the argument. (The winner of the argument is always the one that the author agrees with.) These plays are called "The Dialogues."

Write a "dialogue" between at least two characters. In your dialogue, show your readers what you think of the issue of cosmogony.

Chapter 3
Too many religions

According to the government, the United States has seventy-eight religions. Okay...It probably has more. But there are seventy-eight different religious groups in America that have at least 60,000 members.

That's a lot of religions. Most of us believe that this is a good thing. People should be allowed to believe whatever they want. But that doesn't mean all those religions are *right*, does it?

Imagine a classmate comes up to you and asks you to join his Christian prayer group. You might say something like, "That's okay. I'm Jewish." Imagine that he responds, "Are you sure that your religion is the right one? How do you know that Christianity isn't right and Judaism wrong?"

How would you respond?

As you formulate a retort, consider the following questions. Try marking down the first answers that come to your mind.

1. In order for your religion to be right, do the other ones have to be wrong?
2. Are there some basic truths that all (or most) religions get right?
3. Does it matter to God what religion you believe in?

We asked, *"If there is one God, why are there so many religions?"*

Rachel B.

One of my teachers, Rabbi Zalman Schachter-Shalomi, suggests that we imagine God as a kind of cosmic radio station. God is always "broadcasting"—there's always a stream of revelation and blessing emanating from God.

We're like radio receivers. Some of us may not be "tuned in" to God at all. Some of us make an effort to find God's presence in our lives, or to wake up and notice the presence of God—that's like switching "on." For Jews, studying Torah and observing mitzvot can be ways of receiving the signal God's broadcasting, or training ourselves to be receptive to that signal. For many Jews, Torah itself is the message God broadcasts.

But not all of us are tuned in to the same station. Different people from different cultures and traditions receive messages based on what frequency they're tuned in to. So our Christian cousins might be receiving revelation from God that looks different from the revelation we're getting. Same goes for our Buddhist cousins, and our Hindu cousins, and everybody else you can think of.

We're listening to different channels on the all-day, all-night God broadcast...but the One God is doing all of the broadcasting.

Another way to think of it is through the parable of the blind men and the elephant. Several blind men, the story goes, were introduced to an elephant. The one who felt its tusks thought it was a pointy creature; the one who patted its skin thought it was something big and leathery; the one who touched its mighty leg thought it was something like a tree. All of them were correct—but none of them had the whole picture. The reality of the elephant was grander than their limited senses could imagine. God is like that elephant; each tradition comes away with a part of God's story.

According to Rachel B., how are Buddhists, Hindus, and Christians all our "cousins"?

Isaac

In high school I asked a Catholic friend if she thought I was destined for Hell simply because I am Jewish. Her response surprised me: "You believe in God, and I believe in God; we just call that God by different names. Belief is what matters." The lesson that stems from her words is crucial for the twenty-first century: varying individual beliefs can be based on one universal truth. We often get so caught up in noticing the differences between religions—or, closer to home, in the distinctions between the movements of Judaism—that we forget to notice that below the surface we all believe in the same things. If, as the Torah teaches, we are all created in the image of God, then God must have infinite possibilities. And if so, the paths to God must similarly be endless. Mordecai Kaplan, the founder of Reconstructionism, wrote, "It matters very little how we conceive God as long as we so believe in God that belief in [God] makes a tremendous difference in our lives." As we journey on our individual paths to God, it's important to remember to look out into the world every so often—we might be surprised by what other paths we cross along the way. If we begin to notice these points of intersection, we can begin—finally—to break down some of the barriers between the movements, between religions, and ultimately, between us and God.

For Isaac, does it matter what religion you believe in?

Shira

I believe that God is inherently indefinable, beyond our understanding, and it is the work of our lifetimes to learn how to appreciate, praise, and understand this mystery as best as our senses will allow us to. This is my journey of faith. This journey is available to anyone who chooses it.

The beautiful cultures we are born into use all of their creativity to answer the big questions that come up on our journey. Questions like: Why am I here? What created me? How do I live my life? Answers are different, just as there is amazing diversity in our foods, music, and languages.

Religion is the way culture impacts what our answers sound like, just as it affects what our music sounds like. I personally don't believe there are right or a wrong answers to these big questions. I do believe there are answers that support life and community and answers that do not. Do my answers help me respect others and value my own life? Do my answers help me protect the environment and take care of people unable to take care of themselves? What is important to me about Judaism is not that it's the right answer—it's that it belongs to me, because of the people related to me who protected, struggled with, and loved these answers so much that they kept them in good condition until I was born and ready to inherit them. Anything that important to my great, great, great, on and on grandparents must be valuable. They safeguarded their answers so well that they survived thousands of years of history so they can now help me learn how to live my life more meaningfully.

So my religion, this gift, is the process of billions of my ancestors having beautiful, complicated, meaningful relationships with God. And it's definitely worth my time, love, faith, and energy. I believe everyone should look to see what their culture has beautifully wrapped and presented to them as a way to become a healthy, conscious person of integrity. I love that my religion says there is a Oneness to the entire universe because we are all created by One God. We should not be in conflict, because we are all connected. That there is some good stuff that can hopefully help me figure out how to be a pretty cool person.

According to Shira, why is it that there are so many religions? Are they all right?

Too many religions?

Draw (or illustrate using a computer graphics program) an intellectual map that illustrates the world's religions. Does one religion go in the center? Are they all of equal importance or equal "correctness"? It will probably help to go back to Rachel B., Isaac, and Shira to help figure out your own answers.

Chapter 4
Free will

At 11:19 a.m. on Tuesday, April 20, 1999, two teenagers named Eric Harris and Dylan Klebold walked into Columbine High in Jefferson County, Colorado, and carried out a shooting rampage. The two killed thirteen people—twelve students and one teacher—before killing themselves.

A newspaper reporter is working on a story about religious reactions to tragedies like the Columbine massacre. She calls you and asks, "As a Jew, do you think that what happened at Columbine High School was all part of God's plan?"

As you think about your response to the reporter, jot down your initial answers to the following questions:

1. Do you think that God has a "supreme plan" for the world and that bad things that happen are just part of that plan? Why or why not?

2. Does God know what we're going to do before we do it? If so, do we really have the power to make choices?

3. Does God have the power to intervene in human behavior? If so, do you think God ever uses that power?

We asked, "Do we have free will?"

Jennifer

Have you ever seen a movie reel laid out in front of you? It is fascinating to realize that the movies we watch in the theater in "real time" are basically small individual squares of film that are moving so fast we only *think* it is all one continuous strip. Should the movie reel stop spinning, the picture on the screen would be frozen on one scene. That is the difference between how God sees time and how we do. We see our lives frame-by-frame, moment-by-moment. We are bound by the constraints of worldly time which does not allow us to physically revisit the past or to see into the future. We are forced to live in the present moment at all times (even if we are remembering something that happened yesterday or dreaming about something we hope will happen tomorrow). God, on the other hand, has a very different notion of time. God can take the movie reel, unwind the entire thing, and see it all laid out at the same time (past, present, and future). For God, what happened at Mt. Sinai is just as easily accessible as what is happening in the world right now, and, therefore God can also effortlessly see what is going to happen three thousand years from now. God can see all the choices we are going to make, all the wonderful things that are going to occur, and, unfortunately, all the not-so-great events that will transpire in the future. It is all like one big picture for God, a big picture that we, as human beings, must live piece-by-piece throughout our lives and throughout the generations.

According to Jennifer, do people make their own choices, or did God already make the choices for us?

Justin

Before this question is answered, the question needs to be clarified. If one is asking do we have the ability to think for ourselves, the answer is "yes." However, when we ask do we have autonomy over ourselves, the answer is "no." Our tradition has an understanding that our bodies are not our own but actually belong to the Holy One of Blessing.

If we believe that God is the Creator of all things, then so is our will a creation of God. Therefore all of our actions, done and not done, all of our thoughts, realized and not realized, are due to God being our ultimate Creator.

So the essence of our experience as human beings is only through the lens of God as our Creator and the Judge of All Being. Rabbi Moshe Cordovaero in his work *Tomer Devorah* says, "Without doubt, nothing is hidden from God's providence. In addition, there is not a moment that a person is not nourished and sustained by the Divine power bestowed upon him. This being, no person ever sinned against God without God's self bestowing that person's existence and the ability to move their limbs, at every moment." In other words, even when a person performs actions that would seemingly be unfavorable to God, it is still God's providence, God as Supernal Ruler, who allows a person to perform transgressions.

Our ability to breathe is because of our Creator; our ability to think is because of our Creator; our ability to move is because of our Creator; all we have and all we are is because of our Creator. So while we may not have autonomy over ourselves, because God is the One Sovereign, we have a responsibility to God to act in accordance with God's will, which is, in essence, why our "free will" is but an illusion that the Creator has endowed us with.

According to Justin, how is free will an "illusion"?

Sara

Our lives are a frenzy. We are caught up in a rush of things to do, seeking to control the chaos by planning our lives to the minute. We have hand-held organizers that let us color-code our days and TiVo that makes the TV shows work on our time. We do our best to maintain complete control over our world. The same sometimes goes for our emotions. We manage our stress and manage our anger. We seek love as though it's been hiding from us, and we push ourselves to "get over" past relationships as fast as we can. Even something as primal as emotion is subject to our quest for complete control.

Do we truly have free will, complete control over our actions and emotions? In *Parashat Va-Era* God says that Pharaoh's heart will be hardened, and it is: Pharaoh refuses to let the Jewish people go. Does God really have the power to do this?

Many Jewish thinkers have argued that we do have ownership over our own deeds, and we are responsible for our own conduct. We have the ability to choose: evil over good, or good over evil.

But the hardening of Pharaoh's heart seems to contradict this. God keeps Pharaoh's heart hardened to the plight of the Israelites. Pharaoh does not have the option to choose good.

Is this unique to Pharaoh, or can we, too, lose our carefully sought control? Are we, in fact, *not* the masters of our own destinies?

Later in the Torah portion God instructs Moses to demand that Pharaoh "let my people go that they may worship Me." We know well what God wants. Our ancestors were brought out of slavery so that they could praise God, so that they could eventually learn Torah, and so that they and we could use its lessons to make our choices between good and evil. Let's be honest. We can't say for sure whether or not God steers the actions of our hearts. But we can do our best to choose good of our own accord. As it says in Deuteronomy, *U'Vharta ba-Hayyim*. "Choose life, that you may live." We should hold fast to this teaching, just in case the choice *is* ours to make.

In the end, perhaps we must relinquish total control and admit that we *don't* have all the answers, that we may never know if we are acting of our own free will. But then, we can and we must maintain enough control to be kind, to love God, and to follow our *yetzer tov* (good inclination). As people bound by a Divine covenant, we must behave as if the option is ours, even if we can't know for sure.

According to Sara, what kind of choices should we make "if we can't know for sure" whether or not we have free will?

Dan

Free will is our greatest gift and our biggest curse. It is the source of pride, creativity, and hope, and it is the cause of wars, discrimination, and oppression.

How do we know we have free will? Because you could close this book right now, and no one can stop you. If you are in a classroom, you might get in trouble or be asked to open it back up again, but using our free will means that there are consequences. You can choose to put your hand on a hot stove, but it doesn't mean it's a good idea. Since we have free will and anybody can do what they want, we need to have rules and laws to make sure everyone is safe. For example, you have the freedom to rob someone. If everyone acted on this free will, no one would ever be safe, so we make laws against it. The Torah, in part, is a set of rules to help us use our free will in the best possible way.

If free will did not exist, God could just *make* us follow the rules. For example, imagine that you invented a new game. You can't force people to play the game, and even if you could, they'd probably hate it for being forced to play. However, if you teach them the rules and people choose to play the game on their own, it's a lot more fun for them and much more rewarding for you. In the same way, God doesn't want to force us to follow the laws of the Torah. We are taught the laws, mitzvot, and traditions, and when we *choose* to follow them, it is much more rewarding for us and satisfying for God.

If we do have free will, how can God foresee the future? Maybe it's like when we hang out with our friends or our siblings. Sometimes we know them so well that we already know exactly how they are going to act even before they do.

According to Dan, how is free will "our greatest gift and our biggest curse"?

Did Eric and Dylan have free will?

Write an email to the reporter explaining your beliefs—as a Jew—about free will. Did the Columbine shootings happen because of God's plan? Or were Eric and Dylan (the murderers) acting according to their free will? As you write your email you may want to quote Jennifer, Justin, Sara, or Dan.

Chapter 5

prayer

Imagine you're visiting a friend in the hospital. Your friend is pretty sick.

Usually when people propose hypothetical situations like these they insert the phrase "God forbid." When they do this, they're acknowledging that this is the sort of hypothetical situation that no one likes to deal with. Since this is a book about theology, it would be a little strange to say "God forbid." Here's what we will say: Hopefully, you won't ever be in a situation where you'll have to visit a really sick friend in the hospital. But the reality is that you probably will one day, and maybe you already have. Unfortunately, sicknesses and injuries and other painful things are a part of life. (For more on this kind of morose stuff, see Chapter 10.) Anyway...

Imagine you're visiting a friend in the hospital. Your friend is pretty sick. You're sitting at the bedside, and your friend leans over and whispers something to you.

"Pray with me."

What would you do?

As you consider your possible actions, ponder the following:

1. Have you ever prayed effectively? (And what might it mean to "pray effectively"?)

2. What's the point of prayer?

3. Is prayer more about God, or is it more about the person doing the praying?

4. What kinds of things should people pray for?

We asked, *"Does prayer work?"*

Rachel B.

Does prayer work? That depends on what we mean by "prayer," and also by "work."

Usually when people ask this question they're talking about petitionary prayer (prayer that asks for something, like a new bike, or a good grade, or a sick person to get well). These prayers are worthwhile, in part because they help us understand what it is we want, and in part because it's good to express our needs to God (that's what the bulk of the weekday *amidah* prayer consists of).

But petitionary prayer isn't the only kind of praying we do. Often our prayers are designed to remind us to feel grateful—like the *modeh/modah ani* blessing said in the morning, or like the blessings we say before and after each meal. Often our prayers are designed to remind us that we are not alone, and that we are part of a chain of tradition stretching back for countless generations. This kind of prayer "works" when we engage in it with *kavanah*, heart and intention.

Petitionary prayers aren't always answered the way we want them to be. Maybe we prayed for something that wasn't possible, according to the laws of the reality we live in—like for Hurricane Katrina to vanish before it could hit the Gulf Coast, or for someone who was dying to miraculously recover. Does that mean that the prayer didn't "work," or that God isn't listening? I don't think so. I think one of the tough things about growing up is accepting that prayer doesn't always do what we want it to—but that it can change our lives and strengthen our relationship with God anyway.

I believe that God is always listening, and that our prayers are always answered with love, compassion, and a cosmic "Yes!" But I also believe that "yes" doesn't always look like what we want it to.

In my own life I say a lot of petitionary prayers, but I try to shift them away from pure "gimme." I might pray, "God, please help me get through this." And often I pray, "God, please help me do what I need to do here." If I want things to change in my life, I can and should ask God for help—and I should also take action. Because one of the ways God answers prayer, if you ask me, is by helping us answer it for and with each other and ourselves.

According to Rachel B., what is the role of petitionary prayers?

Justin

The Rambam wrote in his *Mishneh Torah* that "All prayer that is not with intention is not prayer." Prayer is not just reading words; it is feeling them, internalizing them, and realizing them. It is true that we are commanded to pray three times a day, and that the commandments are more to serve God than to serve us. However, we can benefit from them as well. Perhaps more than any other mitzvot, we can derive immense personal gain from prayer. Prayer is meditation. It provides a set amount of time to ignore the external fears and complications of your life and engage in a personal dialogue with God.

Prayer, however, is in the eye of the beholder. If someone reads the words just to read them, that person has not prayed. It is very possible, and even preferable, to pray beyond the words in the prayerbook. Prayer is about not only connection to God, but also connecting to ourselves, to our core. It is time for contemplation and taking account of ourselves. Prayer in Hebrew can be difficult for many since so many of us do not know exactly what we are reading. But praying in Hebrew does more than make us "feel Jewish". It connects us to our heritage and to contemporary Jews everywhere and anywhere in the world.

It could be said that the more one focuses intention toward something, the more easily one could manifest that desire. That is what prayer is for, to allow for us to focus our intention toward God so that we might be more inclined to manifest things for ourselves. Yet it is inappropriate to pray for superficial things; for example, "I pray that my parents buy me a new video game" or "I pray that I get straight As this year in school". Someone who prays for these things has not prayed

41

but merely expressed desire for material gain. It is appropriate to pray for other's well-being and for the health of the world. Whether or not God listens to and heeds our prayers we cannot know, but praying for others reminds us that we are not alone, and that, in turn, has great effect on how we interact with others. If we pray for God to feed the hungry and clothe the needy, we are more likely to feed the hungry and clothe the needy. Therefore, prayer does not inevitably teach us more about God, but it will certainly teach us more about ourselves.

According to Justin, what does intention have to do with praying?

Leah

When I was in college, my mother was diagnosed with a brain tumor and had to undergo five days of intense radiation therapy. Like all believers in modern science, we attacked the problem medically: finding the best doctor, choosing a treatment option, making appointments, etc.

As Jews, we also attacked the problem spiritually. Our rabbi and cantor brought my mother into the sanctuary for a special blessing. Members of our congregation stocked our refrigerator with comfort food, which is always important in the midst of a crisis. We enlisted our non–Jewish friends to pray for my mother in their own places of worship. I prayed at exactly the time of her treatment each day, whether it was in my dorm room or with my own Jewish community at college. My father created a CD of my mother's favorite music and prayers to play during her treatment, including something sung or played by each of her children. My mother recited the *Shema* each time they aimed the radiation beam at her head.

Five years later, my mother is fine. I don't know if this means "prayer works". I'm sure that there have been times that people prayed just as hard as we did and didn't get what they wanted.

However, I believe that prayer was one of many factors that helped my mom to heal and helped my family through a difficult and frightening time. My mom says that everything helped, even the fact that her doctor—who could have said he was too busy saving lives to bother with simple human kindness—took her arm and walked her to the elevator after each of her treatments.

With all we know about science and medicine, some people might say that it's silly to believe that prayer can heal someone. But to me, it's no sillier than saying she got better because a doctor pointed a "laser beam" at her head for an hour each day.

Prayer can work in a lot of ways. It can give a person strength or put that person in the right mind-set to accomplish something important. It can bring people together to comfort and support each other during a difficult time. And maybe, just maybe, it can work because there is Somebody, Somewhere, listening.

According to Leah, in what ways can prayer work?

Rachel K.

Each time I am in a play, there is a great deal of preparation for me to do. I must really get inside my character, figuring out who she is and what makes her tick. I must understand her relationships with the other characters in her world and come to know, both through the script and through improvisation, how she communicates with them. Additionally, I must become comfortable in my character's body: How does she hold herself? How does she move? What does she wear?

Prayer is a lot like acting. The Hebrew verb "to pray"—*lahitpalel*—means "to judge oneself". Through prayer we have the ability to develop ourselves—our characters—into the people we want to be. We pray the timeless lines of the *siddur*—the script—as well as the personal lines—the improvisation—that come from our hearts. Communal prayer enables us to communicate not only with ourselves and God, but also with the other characters on our spiritual stage—our friends and family.

Tallit and *tefillin* are our prayer costumes. They enable us to "get into character," so to speak, helping us to elevate our energy into prayer mode and focusing our minds and our hearts. When I first began wearing *tallit* and *tefillin* it felt like the dress rehearsal. I wasn't completely comfortable in the prayer garb. I couldn't figure out how to keep my *tallit* on my shoulders, and I never seemed to wrap my *tefillin* tightly enough. As time went on I became more comfortable in these costumes. Now each time I put them on I strive to be in my "best character," and I hope that my prayer will be like a successful opening night. Truth be told, sometimes it is, and sometimes it isn't.

Prayer can work in profound and meaningful ways. Through the act of prayer we strive to mold ourselves into better people. Through prayer we connect with our communities and with God. But often prayer is not easy! Sometimes connection happens, and other times we feel completely distracted. But I believe, despite the challenges, that it is vital for us to continue to engage the prayer process, because it is through this very process that we truly can achieve a unique and holy connection—one worthy of a standing ovation.

According to Rachel K., what can we learn from the word "l'hitpalel"?

Prayer Writing

In many synagogues, someone leading the service (or sometimes someone in the congregation) includes a thoughtful English addition to the regular Hebrew service. These little vignettes are sometimes called *kavvanot* or *iyyunim* or simply "meditations." Basically, they're prayers.

Write a *kavvanah* for services at your synagogue. As you write, consider: Is this a prayer to God? How might people benefit from hearing your prayer? What's the purpose of your prayer?

As you write, you may want to consult with Rachel B., Rachel K, Leah, and Justin.

Chapter 6
Chosenness

If you had a bat or bar mitzvah ceremony, you definitely know the Torah blessings. One of them goes like this:

Barukh Atah Adonai, Eloheinu melekh ha-olam, asher bahar banu mikol ha-amim v'natan lanu at torato. Barukh Atah Adonai, noten ha-Torah.

"Blessed are You, Adonai our God, Ruler of the Universe, who has chosen us from among the peoples, and given us the Torah. Blessed are you, Adonai, who gives the Torah."

Reconstructionist Jews don't say these Torah blessings. Reconstructionism rejects the idea that God chose the Jewish people. The idea of being chosen, according to Reconstructionsim, is a problem because it implies that we are separate and different and better than everyone else.

Imagine that a Reconstructionist Jew—someone about your age who grew up as a member of a Reconstructionist synagogue—is a guest in your congregation. The person asks you, "Why do you say those Torah blessings? Don't they bother you?"

[If you belong to a Reconstructionist synagogue, think about how you might explain the different Torah blessings to someone who is more familiar with Reform or Conservative prayers.]

As you think about how to respond, think about these questions:

1. Why do we remember being "the chosen people" when we read Torah?
2. When might the idea of being "chosen" be a useful idea in which to believe? When might it be particularly hard?

47

3. What are some different ways we can understand what it means to be "chosen"?

We asked, *"Are Jews the Chosen People?"*

Lisa

Our sages say that the world stands on three things: Torah, worship, and loving-kindness. Jews can describe their feeling of chosenness through these three things. Claiming that we are the chosen people does not make us superior to other groups of people; it just gives us more responsibilities in the way that we live. We express our chosenness through Torah, by reading it and following the commandments that are set out for us specifically. Not all Jews choose to express their Judaism through following all of the commandments in the same way that we read them from the Torah.

We also fulfill our chosenness through worship or prayer. Our sacred language is Hebrew, and we feel the need to preserve and learn this language as a special part of being Jewish. You may feel you are suffering through Hebrew school, but the end result is that you will be connected with Jews all over the world just by being able to say our most basic prayers in Hebrew.

The third way that we express our chosenness is through loving-kindness. We have placed a high claim on social justice in the United States and around the world. We are chosen to continue our action to make the world a better place. We make ourselves aware of those who cannot help themselves because we are commanded to love our neighbor as ourselves, *v'ahavta l'reyakha kamokha*. Many times in our history we have been in the position of needing help, so we understand that extending a hand to others is not just something nice to do, but something that is required of us. Our sages have given us this simple statement to remind us of our chosen responsibility to God, to prayer, and to each other.

According to Lisa, how can Jews be "the chosen people"?

Isaac

For generation upon generation Jews have declared themselves to be chosen by God to be *or la goyim*—a light unto the nations. In contemporary America, however, where many of us no longer believe in a supernatural God that literally performs miracles and wonders, it is inconsistent to maintain that we are supernaturally chosen by that same (nonexistent) God. Even more, for Jews living in the twenty-first century, the concept of one group being chosen over and above another is at odds with our American ideal of equality for all. Yet there are still many within our community who cling to the belief, as stated in the *Aleinu*, that "God did not make us like the other nations, did not place us with the peoples of the earth, and did not make our daily lot or our destiny like theirs." The insinuation here (which has been made explicit for many generations) is that the Jews are a people not only separate, but better than all others. Such an invidious distinction, as Judith Plaskow calls it, can play no role in a fair or universal religion. Realizing that such distinctions serve to build barriers as opposed to breaking them down, bringing us further from godliness instead of closer to it, we would do well to rethink our need to be chosen. Perhaps it would be better, instead, to think of ourselves as the "choosing people"—choosing to build a religion that is universal, deeply ethical, and open to all.

According to Isaac, why and how should we re-interpret the idea of being chosen?

Danya

There's a midrash that suggests that when God gave the Torah to Israel on Sinai, God "translated it into seventy languages, so that all the nations might hear." In other words, Jews were given the Torah—a guidebook for living in relationship to God, a set of rules to follow, and a model for how to behave with one another. And that the Jews were, without question, "chosen" by God for this Torah and this covenant and these mitzvot. However, it also means that God gave different kinds of guidebooks to everyone else in the world, written in languages—both literal and metaphoric—that they could understand. Rather than buying into the smug idea that "chosenness" means that Jewish people are God's pet nation, I think this midrash is telling us that God "chose" different peoples for connecting to the sacred in different ways, and we can't necessarily understand the guides that weren't written for us. Which isn't to say we shouldn't try to understand the people reading them—that's most certainly part of our work.

We all move within concentric circles: First we learn to see ourselves as individuals, then as members of a family, and then, Judaism reminds us, we're members of a people as well. But if we stop there and don't see ourselves as part of the human race, then we're missing the final jump, learning how to identify with everyone and seeing each other as part of our shared, beautiful, messy humanity as a whole. We are all created in the Divine image, after all, and to know one another is, in its way, to know God.

According to Danya, what does it mean to be "the chosen people"?

Explaining "Chosen"

Imagine that a Reconstructionist Jew—someone about your age who grew up as a member of a Reconstructionist synagogue—is a guest in your congregation. The person asks you, "Why do you say those Torah blessings? Don't they bother you?"

[If you belong to a Reconstructionist synagogue, think about how you might explain the different Torah blessings to someone who is more familiar with Reform or Conservative prayers.]

Write down how you might respond to this guest. Make sure that your response is really based on what *you* believe, not only on what your synagogue's ideology might be.

Chapter 7
Biblical truth

During Passover in 2001 Rabbi David Wolpe, a Conservative rabbi at Sinai Temple in Los Angeles, stood before his congregation and gave three sermons in which he said that the Exodus from Egypt didn't happen the way the Torah says it did.

"The truth is that virtually every modern archeologist who has investigated the story of the Exodus, with very few exceptions, agrees that the way the Bible describes the Exodus is not the way it happened, if it happened at all," Wolpe told his congregants.

The sermons sparked a lot of controversy.

Dennis Prager, a Jewish author and radio talk-show host, wrote an essay declaring that Wolpe was wrong. "If the Exodus did not occur, there is no Judaism. Judaism stands on two pillars—Creation and Exodus," Prager wrote. "Judaism no more survives the denial of the Exodus than it does the denial of the Creator."

Lots of rabbis in Los Angeles and all over the country spoke out for or against Wolpe's sermons. Lots of people wrote letters to Los Angeles newspapers.

If you had been sitting in services that day, what would you have thought?

As your formulate your answer, think about the following questions. If you have any reactions, you should jot them down.

1. Why do you think Rabbi Wolpe's sermons got people so riled up?
2. Does it matter whether or not the Bible is true? Why or why not?
3. Who wrote the Bible?

We asked, *"Is the Bible true?"*

Joel S.

Yes!

Oh, I'm sorry...what did you mean by true? Did a man called Moses really lead a people called the Children-of-Israel out of a place called Egypt? Did God really talk to us or really perform all those miracles? Sorry, I can't answer those questions. Neither can anyone else beyond a shadow of your doubt.

But I would respond to these questions with one of my own. Can the Bible still be meaningful even if NONE of the recorded stories ever really happened? We've got to redefine the word "true". Where the Bible is "true" is in its illumination of God-to-Human and Human-to-Human relationships. Whether or not we can historically prove any of our stories in the Bible, we can certainly learn deeply about ourselves and our purpose on this planet. THAT is truth, baby!

The power of reading the Bible Jewishly is that we go beyond a fundamental (literal) understanding of the words. The first time I read the Bible I thought that the beginning was pretty clear: "In the beginning..." But a great teacher and commentator, Rashi, wrote that this first verse is far from clear and actually screams, "EXPLAIN ME!" Then he gave his interpretation on what the words mean and how they made the cut as the opener for the Bible. Over the course of the next thousand years many other Jews have read and studied the Bible and provided us with their unique commentaries on what different verses and stories mean.

Our teachers believe in *shivim panim la-Torah* (the seventy faces of the Torah). This means that there are tons of different ways to understand the words of the Bible. If two ways seem to contradict each other, then it just means that they are meant to teach two different ideas. Our rabbis were comfortable with arguments as long as they were *L'Shem Shamayim* (for the sake of heaven). The Bible is our instrument

54

to understand our Creator. To limit it to one "truth" would be to limit God. The more opinions, the greater our understanding of God, the greater the chance to find "truth."

If you want "truth," it's in the Bible, just not the way you might think. SEARCHING for "truth" is meaningful, and the Bible is a great place to start. Don't ask me if the Exodus really happened; ask me WHY it happened.

According to Joel S., how can we understand the Bible from so many different—even contradictory—perspectives?

Josh L.

Only after reading Macbeth in tenth grade did I really appreciate Shakespeare. I had read other Shakespeare before, and I had seen a few movies based on his work, but something clicked with Macbeth. Probably I had become comfortable with his English, which at first had felt like a foreign language. The next year I learned about the controversy surrounding his life, his existence, and the possibility that he did not write the plays attributed to his name. Because there is not much historical data about his life, many scholars look at his language and syntax and compare it to other writers and create a whole host of theories about his life or the life of the "real" writer.

Would the quality of Shakespeare's poetry and plays be diminished if it were discovered that someone else or a group of writers actually authored the works attributed to him? Romeo and Juliet would still be the greatest love story ever told! The political intrigue in Hamlet would still ring true today. There is literature in this world whose origins transcend proof, its meaning screaming the truth. This is also the case with Torah. The Torah is True, not because it is an accurate historical account or because it was written by God (I cannot prove either of those points), but because the Jewish tradition accepts it as the basis for its religion. For 3,000 years, beginning with the Prophets and continuing with the Rabbis in Babylon, the medieval Jewish philosophers, the Kabbalists, the Hasidim, the early Reformers in Germany, and modern Jews like rabbis Leo Beck, Mordechai Kaplan, Joseph Soloveitchik, and Ovadia Yosef, the Torah has been the starting point for the Jews. The Torah is an amazing document that extends beyond the boundaries of literature, legal document, instruction book. It is the currency that Jews use for conversation. I do not think it matters whether or not the Torah happened; it matters what you do with it. Some people say that God wrote the Torah, and that is why they do mitzvot. For them, the Torah's authority is that it is the word of God. Other people say that the Torah was written by people, it is recorded folklore, and therefore they do not do mitzvot. I do not buy either of these arguments. I appreciate biblical scholarship that uncovers the development of the Torah, trying to develop the story of how the Torah was written, and so the authority of the Torah is not simply its author. But I also believe that one should observe mitzvot. Even if the Torah is recorded folklore (which I reject), it is *our* folklore and has been the starting point for the Jewish experience for 3,000 years.

According to Josh L., how are the Bible and Shakespeare similar? How are they different?

Danya

I have a confession to make: I don't actually care whether or not the Bible is historically accurate, or if "what really happened" even conforms to traditional Jewish beliefs. I love learning about new scholarly theories and archeological findings—I geeked out on them before I ever became religious, and when I began to believe in God, I saw no need to start disproving them. Rather, as I came to the Torah with a new kind of curiosity, I started to see that the stories in the Torah were metaphors for the spiritual states I'd already been experiencing for some time.

Even if I'd never actually wrestled with an angel the way Jacob did, I'd certainly struggled with the idea of God, and with the part of me that craved holiness even if the rest of me didn't want to be bothered. I'd never seen a burning bush, but I'd certainly been startled by a luminous sense of radiance, and, like Moses, gotten bit freaked out when it seemed that paying attention to that sense might have major implications for what I was going to do with my life. The book of Kings talks about the "still, small voice" of God that can be heard after all of the chaos of the world quiets down—isn't that familiar to everyone? As Rabbi Alan Lew put it, "The Torah is the record of the human encounter with God—the transcendent, the absolute. Every page of the Torah either describes this encounter or prepares us for it or discusses its implications."

It's clear to me that the Torah is true on the most primal, human level—hidden inside its stories are whispers of who God is and what God is like, powerful lessons about how we can live in connection to the Divine and how to best take care of ourselves and each other. It doesn't actually matter to me whether the words of the Torah were actually authored by God Godself, by people who had a deeply spiritual experience of God, or even just by people with the regular agendas of their time and place. Maybe some combination of all three things? I'll never know for sure, in any case, and I don't think that it ultimately matters. Whether Abraham and Moses were real people or "just" literary figures doesn't change the power of their stories and the fact that we can read them over and over and always learn something new from them. The Torah gleams of truth, wisdom, and the sacred in a way that mere history can never touch.

According to Danya, how is the Torah even more "true" than history?

Sadie

God wrote the Torah. The Torah is comprised of five books: *Bereishit, Shemot, Va-Yikra, Ba-Midbar,* and *D'varim.* Actually, the traditional Jewish view is that God spoke the Torah to Moses on the top of Mount Sinai, and Moses wrote it down.

This idea shouldn't be new to you. We say it all the time: "*V'zot ha-Torah asher sam Moshe lifnei b'nei Yisrael, al pi Adonai, b'Yad Moshe.*" These are the words chanted, in Jewish synagogues all over the world, at the end of the Torah service as the scroll is lifted on high and admired. Where does this tradition originate? This idea comes directly from the text itself. Five times (and in five different places) the Torah says that "God gave the Torah to Moses" (Exodus 17:14, 24:4, 34:27; Deuteronomy 31:9, 31:24–26).

Let me be clear: I believe that the laws, the stories, and the traditions are all directly from God.

Does it matter where the Torah comes from? I would answer "Yes!"

To me it is important that the source of my Judaism—the foundation of my religion, its beliefs, rituals, laws, and stories—comes from something/someone greater than any human being or group of people. Yes, the Torah is old and has been passed down for hundreds of generations, but just because something is ancient does not give it the power to be foundational for an entire religion. Rather, I believe that the source of Judaism, the Torah, comes from the source of life itself, God. A doctrine written by God is worth preserving, even when it seems outdated and not applicable in our lives. Because it was written by God, we as Jews have the obligation to preserve the text with integrity and to struggle with how this ancient, truly divine doctrine still applies in our lives today.

According to Sadie, why is it important to believe that the Torah is a factually true document written by God?

Biblically Speaking

Imagine you're sitting in Rabbi Wolpe's congregation. It is Passover, and the year is 2001. (Think about how much you love matzah. Mmm. Matzah.)

What do you think when you hear his sermon? And what do you think in the following days when he becomes the center of controversy?

Write a letter to the local newspaper explaining what it was like to hear Rabbi Wolpe say what he said, and discuss your own opinions and beliefs about the Bible's truth (or lack thereof).

Conversations with God

In Biblical times God talked to people. A lot. God talked to Adam and Noah, to Avram (and then Abraham) and Sara, to Isaac and Rebecca, to Jacob and Rachel and Leah. God talked to Moses a ton.

We consider these people to be important role models and heroes. We talk about *Avraham Avinu* and *Moshe Rabbeinu*, Abraham our father and Moses our teacher.

Things are different in our own times. If you've ever heard someone say "God talks to me" or "God made me do it," it's probably the type of person we regard as crazy, or at least a little off-kilter.

It's harder for us to accept that God talks to people in our own time than it is to accept that God spoke to our spiritual ancestors.

Have you ever had a conversation with God? What was it like? If you haven't, what would it be like if you could sit down and talk with God?

As you reflect on these questions, consider the following:

1. Why might people *want* to have a conversation with God?

2. Why do we think it's so weird to talk to God? What changed between biblical times and today?

3. Is it possible that God used to talk to people but has since stopped? Why or why not?

We asked, "Does God speak to people?" (or "Why did God stop talking to people?")

Rachel B.

God spoke to me once. It was a Friday morning; I'd been on retreat all week, studying Jewish meditation and texts about *tikkun olam* (healing the world), and I was out walking during *shaḥarit* (morning service). We'd been instructed to take some time to walk alone and speak out loud to God—like a personalized *amidah* prayer.

I felt a little bit silly talking out loud to God, but I did it anyway. In the distance I could see others doing the same thing I was: walking in the fields or around the herb and flower garden. I said, "So. Um. God. Hi." There was silence.

I said, "It's been really nice spending this week with You." The leaves rustled in the breeze. "I didn't realize how much I missed You, actually." Talking out loud to God was getting easier. "I can't believe in two more days I'm going home, back to my regular life where I don't have the time—or I guess I don't make the time—to pray three times a day—where I don't have this kind of community. Where I feel like You're far away." I blurted out, "I wish I could take You home with me."

And all of a sudden I knew, as surely as I knew anything, that God had heard me...and that of course God was going home with me...and that God had been with me all along. God was wrapped around me as lovingly and firmly as the folds of my *tallit*. I realized I was crying, but they were happy tears. "Thanks," I whispered. It felt like the universe was smiling back at me, a little bit amused and filled with boundless love.

How did Rachel B. know that God had heard her?

Josh L.

I have encountered many people who have heard the direct word of God. Generally, these people are standing in the middle of busy public places shouting at the top of their lungs about the end of the world. They appear haggard and dirty, and most of us consider them crazy!

There are religions that believe in a continued literal revelation, for example the Mormons, and this seems like a much greater problem. If one believes that God still speaks to people—that you can actually hear the word of God—then literal revelation still exists! There are several problems that arrive with this view. Firstly, many of these so-called prophecies go against what is written in the Torah; they reject previously held notions in order to change the status quo. The fake prophets making these claims use the name of God to sound more authoritative. Moreover, if God spoke to people, there would be absolute anarchy. I would not be responsible to the people around me, my community, or my government, because I could claim that the ultimate authority has given me a stamp of approval for my actions.

What makes the Jewish tradition so magnificent is the layers of interpretation that have accumulated. These layers of interpretation provide us with multiple entrances into the text as different Jews said different things depending on the time and place they wrote. These layers can also be difficult for us to digest, as they can weigh heavily on our minds. It can be tiring to sift through all the different commentary that has accumulated throughout history to reach comfort with a text. But what our tradition does afford us is the opportunity if not the responsibility to constantly *osek b'Torah*, to get our hands messy with interpretation. "Turn it and turn it and turn it again," we learn in *Mishnah Avot*. God may not literally speak to us; however, we are constantly uncovering and unfolding new meaning when we learn Torah.

According to Josh L., how can we "talk" to God?

Rachel K.

David lived in a little town in Poland. Each Shabbos he would watch as numerous young men filed into the rebbe's home for the Friday night meal. David would peek through the windows and watch as the dining room filled up with people. At first it seemed they were just eating and talking, but then things got a little weird. David would watch as the rebbe's guests began to move their bodies in awkward ways, swaying, jumping, and swinging their limbs to and fro. Finally one week, after Shabbat, David mustered the courage to visit the rebbe and ask him what this strange Shabbat experience was all about. He approached the rebbe nervously. "Holy rebbe," he said, "each Shabbos I watch as guests pile into your home. And each Shabbos I peer through the window and see them moving their bodies about in ways I just don't understand."

The rebbe looked up at David. He realized David's problem—David was spending Shabbos looking through the window, but he had never stepped inside. Although David could see the guest's movements through this window, he could not hear the singing, so he did not realize that the guests were dancing. David could not hear the music.

So often we go through our lives looking through the window. Instead we need to tear down the walls that separate us from the real event. Only when we are on the inside—when we are really present in each and every moment—can we truly hear God's music. We hear these holy melodies within our relationships with friends and family, the call to social justice, and the magic of Torah, mitzvot, and prayer. It is in this fabulous, complex, and challenging music that we hear God's voice in our time.

According to Rachel K., how is it that we can "hear God's voice"?

God Talk

Have a conversation with God. Go ahead. Try it.

What should you say to God? What would you ask? How would God answer? What would God ask you, and how would you answer?

Script your conversation with God. Write out your part of the conversation, and record what God says (or would say) to you.

Chapter 9
Miracles

Every Hanukkah we say blessings over the candles. The second blessing says the following:

Blessed are You, Adonai, sovereign of the Universe, Who made miracles for our ancestors in those days at this time.

Imagine you have a non–Jewish friend over to celebrate Hanukkah with you and your family. After hearing the blessing they ask what it means and then ask, "Do you really believe that God makes miracles like oil burning and seas parting? We haven't seen any miracles like that recently."

As you consider how you might respond, think about these questions:

1. How, exactly, would you define the word "miracle"?

2. Do you think that God used to make miracles? How do you know?

3. Do you think God still makes miracles? How do you know?

We asked, "Does God make miracles?"

Justin

Somehow, people want something outrageous and spectacular with their miracles. What are the miracles that Jews usually think of? The Flood, the Revelation of Torah, the splitting of the sea, the Passover, the oil burning for eight days that we celebrate at Hanukkah, the victory of the Jews at Shushan that we celebrate at Purim. Therefore, when we fail to see these "great" miracles, we say miracles don't happen at all! But what of the small miracles that people miss every day?

Perhaps a distinction between the miracles mentioned above and the small miracles could be public and private. The miracles of Revelation and Hanukkah were public miracles for all of Israel. But we all experience miracles every day that nobody else will ever see or experience. Sometimes they are small; sometimes they are big. We've all heard stories of people surviving unbelievable events like accidents or perilous journeys. I myself have had one of those experiences, and it is actually the very reason that I began observing mitzvot. I suffer from a not-uncommon skin ailment called eczema, which manifests itself in very itchy rashes and sometimes open sores. These sores, in my case, became infected, and I contracted a staphylococcus infection, which eventually infected my entire bloodstream and my entire body. This infection got so bad that I was forced to stay in bed for a very long time, and it was difficult to do simple tasks like dress myself. After being helped through this process by loved ones I had to be at a hospital for more intensive care. One afternoon the doctor came in when I was much healthier and told me that statistically speaking I should be blind, paralyzed, or possibly dead; that people who are that infected for as long as I was do not survive unscathed, but I did. I cannot accept that miracles do not happen.

The Midrash teaches us that when the Children of Israel were at the splitting of the sea, two of them ran into the water before it had even begin to split. One jumped back and was disgusted by the mud; the other kept running until the water was up to his nose, so great was his faith in God, and it wasn't until he could hardly stand anymore that the sea split. The rest of the people would have missed that miracle were it not for that one individual's belief in the miracle. Miracles are what we make of them, and unless we look for them, we will miss them every day.

According to Justin, how are public and private miracles different? How are they similar?

Leah

A few years ago I spent the summer as a chaplain on a neurological floor at a hospital. People on that floor were living normal lives until the day they started having seizures or had a stroke. A malfunction in the tiniest receptors in their brains made it so they were suddenly unable to walk, speak, or see. They had to spend days lying in the dark, hooked up to electrodes that monitored their brain activity, or even undergoing frightening surgical procedures. We never realize how important, how miraculous each little mechanism in our bodies is...until one of them stops working.

Many people think that God doesn't make miracles anymore. We don't see seas part and mountains move they way they do in the stories of the Bible. A miracle may not always be the kind of miracle you read about in the Bible. In our prayer service we usually think of miracles when we sing *Mi Khamokha,* the prayer about the miracle of the parting of the Red Sea.

Sometimes we don't understand that it is a huge miracle every morning that we wake up, breathe in, open our eyes, stand up, and even go to the bathroom. There are blessings for many of these activities, believe it or not. One of these blessings is called *Asher Yatzar.* Its words thank God for making our bodies work each morning, basically saying,

"Thank you for keeping my openings open and my closings closed, because if You didn't, I wouldn't be here." That may not seem like a huge miracle. However, you might think differently if you, or anyone who is close to you, ever experienced life without one of these tiny miracles.

I think about how miraculous our bodies are whenever my grandmother's hearing aids are "on the fritz". With arthritic hands she scoops them out of her ears and starts tinkering with their buttons and dials, taking the batteries out and putting them back in again. My grandmother tells anyone who will listen that she's an atheist, but at these moments she slips: "I don't know if there's a God." She taps on one hearing aid and prepares to put it back in her ear. "But Whoever designed the human ear must have been some kind of genius. Because no one, not even the most brilliant doctors and scientists, can completely duplicate its function."

According to Leah, what does Asher Yatzar *teach us about miracles?*

Rachel K.

"The sun came out!" exclaims my two-year-old daughter Noa as I lift her out of her crib. It is a normal Thursday morning, 7 a.m., and my daughter notices the very same astronomical phenomenon that I have come to take for granted—the sun came out! Noa says this every morning with great glee, as if she didn't expect that the sun would, yet again, grace the sky with its beautiful presence. Before Noa's birth I had given up on miracles. "God doesn't intervene in our lives like that," I would say. "I don't believe in that kind of God." Now that I see the world through the eyes of a two-year-old child, I realize that there are miracles all around us...the flowers that bloom in the spring, the birth of a healthy baby, the feeling of love that exists between two people...and yes, the sun that rises each morning and brightens the sky. Our entire existence is a miracle. However, the true miracle is our ability to recognize and acknowledge these amazing occurrences with wonder and awe.

What did Noa teach Rachel K. about miracles?

Miracles

"Paper-tear midrash" (or "handmade midrash") is a method that allows people—even people who aren't so good at art—to think artistically about difficult abstract stuff. It was invented by Jo Milgrom, who teaches that using the artistic parts of our brain can help us to understand those ideas and concepts (especially in the Torah) that are the hardest to grasp.

Here are the rules. You can use colored construction paper. You can use glue. You can't use anything else. No scissors, no pencils or pens or crayons or markers. You can tear the paper into any kind of pieces you want, and you can glue the paper. That's all.

Using this method—and using only construction paper and glue—do your best to illustrate your definition of the word "miracle."

As you begin to work you may want to consult with the ideas and images suggested by Justin, Leah, and Rachel K.

Theodicy

Imagine that you're walking down the street and you see a crime being committed or an accident happening that you can do something about. Something bad is going to happen, and you have the power to prevent it. In most cases, isn't it your moral obligation to do something? If we have the power to easily prevent suffering, isn't our doing so imperative?

And does the same logic apply to God?

For a lot of people, theodicy is the hardest question about God. That's probably for two reasons. First, people have a hard time thinking rationally about theology when human suffering is involved. Second, theodicy is one of those questions that doesn't lead to satisfying answers.

Theodicy is a fancy word for a simple problem. Let's accept for now that God is all-powerful. God is capable of doing pretty much anything God pleases. Let's also accept that God is good. God isn't interested in having innocent people suffer for no reason. Those two premises come into conflict like this: How can a good God permit so many bad things to happen to good people? If God has the power to stop evil, isn't it wrong for God to let evil—at least the really big and bad forms of evil—exist?

How can we believe in God when there is so much suffering in the world?

How can we believe in a God who permitted the Holocaust to happen?

As you challenge yourself with the question of theodicy, think about the following questions:

1. Can you conceive of a God who is not all-powerful?

2. Can you conceive of a God who is not all good?

3. After the Holocaust, many survivors decided they could not believe in God. At the same time, others realized that they felt more dedicated to their belief in God than before. Why do you think this happened?

We asked, "*How can a good God let bad things happen?*"

Jennifer

When I was fifteen years old, during the summer after my freshman year of high school, two men that I highly admired and respected were severely injured in a car accident. The men were left in hospital beds, and I was left with painful theological questions that demanded from God an answer to that very question: "How could You have let this happen?" The personal answer I have come up with to help me deal with that situation and others like it that I have encountered is that God is omnipotent (all-powerful), omniscient (all-knowing), and benevolent (completely good), but that God has put limits on His power. When the world was created, certain natural laws were established—laws of inertia, gravity, science, math, etc. These laws usually protect us and enable us to make sense of our world. They allow us to accurately predict the outcome and consequences of our physical actions—if you jump from a tree, you are going to fall to the ground; if you are driving a car and do not hit the brake pedal, the car will keep moving until it runs into something; if diseased cells grow inside a body, that person is going to get sick. These are laws that God has chosen to not allow Himself to break, because if God were to break them for one person, God would have to keep on breaking them for everybody, and then our world would become chaotic and unpredictable. God also cannot intervene all the time to stop bad things from happening without taking away our free will (the ability we have to make rational choices concerning our actions). Free will is one of the unique things that make us human, and if we did not have it, all of our choices would already be made for us, and we would not get a say in how our own lives play out. So although God has all the power in the world, and even though God *wants* only good things to happen to us, God has chosen to give us a world where laws and free will enable us to live our lives in a relatively orderly manner. We may choose to put those laws to poor use, or we may decide to use our free will to hurt others, and God (by His self-limiting constraints on His power) cannot stop that from happening; but I believe that God always *hopes* that we make the right choices with the power that *we* are given.

According to Jennifer, what does free will have to do with theodicy?

Danya

Contrary to popular belief, God is neither Santa Claus nor Zeus. The Divine, the all-encompassing Force of Life, is not an angry man sitting in the sky, making lists of whether you've been good or bad and getting ready to punish accordingly. Rather, the answer to "Why do bad things happen do good people?" often has more to do with human beings than with some Divine decree.

In the Garden of Eden story God gives human beings the ability to choose freely—Adam and Eve could eat the fruit or not, but either way they'd have to face the consequences of their decisions. We've been using that free will ever since, and our choices have both intended and unintended outcomes—despite the impulse of many to blame all human suffering on God. For example, what if the reason a person gets cancer is not that he or she personally has done something wrong, but because we as a nation and a globe have poisoned our air, our water, and our food with toxic chemicals and negligence? Are the tsunami and the hurricanes a sign that entire sections of the world were filled with sinners, or a tragic by-product of global warming? Do wars happen because God is angry, or because we humans haven't yet figured out how to work out our problems by non-violent means? Much more is in our control than we often care to admit. The reality of God's existence doesn't take away from the free will we've been using all along.

As unnerving as this idea may be, in another way it's kind of heartening. After all, if free will is so powerful, we might be able to use it for the power of good—to help alleviate some of the misery already out there, or to prevent further harm. We can be responsible for causing good things to happen to all people—we just have to choose to make it happen.

According to Danya, how is the question of theodicy more about human beings than it is about God?

Dan

When David was first learning how to ride a bike, his dad held onto the seat and ran alongside to help him balance. Eventually David's father let go, and David continued riding on his own. After a few feet David lost his balance and fell to the hard pavement. Cut up and bruised, David ran back to his father crying and shouting, "How could you let me fall? It really hurts!"

His father replied, "I'm really sorry, David. I hate to see you get hurt, but if I didn't let go, you'd never learn to ride the bike on your own. Part of learning to ride a bike is falling, getting hurt, and getting right back on the bike."

Sometimes God lets us get hurt so that we can learn and grow. Even if it seems bad at the time, it is actually for a good cause.

According to Dan's metaphor, who does David represent? Who does David's father represent?

Talking Theodicy With Elie Wiesel

Elie Wiesel is a Holocaust survivor who became an author after the war. You may be familiar with his first and most famous book, *Night*. *Night* is basically Wiesel's memoir, his account of what happened to him during the Holocaust.

In the book Wiesel discusses how he struggled with theology while he was a prisoner at Auschwitz-Birkenau, the Nazi concentration and death camp. One day a young boy was hanged, and the other prisoners were forced to walk in front of his dead body and look at the hanging corpse. Wiesel wrote:

> Behind me, I heard [a] man asking: Where is God now? And I heard a voice within me answer him: ...Here He is—He is hanging here on this gallows.

Soon after, the other prisoners attempted to celebrate Rosh ha-Shanah. Wiesel had trouble taking part.

> Blessed be God's name? Why, but why would I bless Him? Every fiber in me rebelled. Because He caused thousands of children to burn in His mass graves? Because He kept six crematoria working day and night, including Sabbath and the Holy Days? Because in His great might, He had created Auschwitz, Birkenau, Buna, and so many other factories of death? How could I say to Him: Blessed be Thou, Almighty, Master of the Universe, who chose us among all nations to be tortured day and night, to watch as our fathers, our mothers, our brothers end up in the furnaces?...But now, I no longer pleaded for anything. I was no longer able to lament. On the contrary, I felt very strong. I was the accuser, God the accused. My eyes had

opened and I was alone, terribly alone in a world without
God, without man.

Write a letter to Elie Wiesel. Respond to him, explaining your own
thoughts on the issue of theodicy. As you write you may want to
consult Jennifer, Danya, and Dan.

Chapter 11

Human Behavior

In many cities in the United States the police have set up cameras at intersections. These "traffic cams" are set to take pictures right when the light turns red. When the cameras capture a car running a red light, a computerized system automatically reads the car's license plate and sends a traffic ticket to the person who owns the car.

Some people have gotten very upset about these cameras. They don't like the idea that computers are watching their every move.

Does God work in the same way? Is God interested in what people do, and does God watch us to make sure we're doing it? Does God reward people who behave correctly and punish people who don't?

As you think about these questions, consider the following:

1. If God cares about human behavior, how do we figure out how to act in the "right" way?

2. How would we know whether or not God rewards and punishes people for their behavior?

3. If God doesn't care about our behavior, should we care about "right" and "wrong"?

We asked, *"Does God care about my behavior?"*

Justin

The Torah is filled with injunctions to observe commandments, and various rewards and punishments are delineated if we do or do not, such as rain and drought. The Prophets are rife with admonitions not to perform empty rituals, and that it is truly justice that God seeks—not the performance of mitzvot without concern for the poor and needy. Today we no longer live in an agrarian society, so the threats of drought do not speak to us. Therefore many have focused on the preaching of the prophets rather than the blessings and curses of the Torah.

Yet does God truly want us to seek justice and also to ignore mitzvot? Quite the contrary. God wants us to seek justice through mitzvot. Some of the commandments in our tradition are logical and forthright. For example, it is obvious why we need to give *tzedakah* to the poor or treat the stranger the same as we would treat family. So do commandments that seemingly have no logical purpose, like *tefillin* or the observance of *kashrut,* have no place? Rather, we should not understand the mitzvot as something that we can quantify or qualify in how they benefit our own lives. The mitzvot are not for us; they are for God.

We human beings are all reflections of one another; we are all one, and all of our actions cause reactions in the world. The Sages said that every time a person does a good deed, a messenger of God is created with a positive purpose in the world. Likewise, every time a person does a bad deed, a messenger of God is created with a negative purpose in the world. And they even said that when a person does a good deed with bad ramifications, or a bad deed with good ramifications, a messenger of God is created with a mixed purpose in the world. This teaches us to always focus our energy toward good deeds so that we fill the world with positive energy and light shines in the world. We adequately reflect one another when we act in love and honesty. We reflect God in the world by performing mitzvot. In this way, treating others well and performing mitzvot go hand in hand in manifesting God in the world.

According to Justin, what is the role of mitzvot in our relationship with God?

Uri

Rava, a fourth-century Babylonian rabbi, writes that there are six questions a person is asked when God judges him or her.

"Did you conduct your worldly affairs in a righteous manner?"

"Was lifelong learning a priority?"

"Did you engage yourself in the raising of children?"

"Were you an optimist?"

"Did you use wise judgment?"

"Did you understand and search for the deeper meaning and hidden meaning of life?" (Babylonian Talmud, *Masekhet Shabbat*)

These questions give us a plan for how we are supposed to live our lives in order to be judged favorably by God. We should be fair in business. We should value our traditions and strive to deepen our learning all the days of our lives. We should raise children responsibly and lovingly (he probably meant within the context of marriage and a family, so wait till you are out of high school for this one). We should always look for the silver lining, even when times look the darkest. We should make wise decisions, carefully weighing all sides of an argument. Finally, we should understand and search for a deeper meaning within our routines so as to elevate our daily lives into the realm of the Holy.

Excuse me, but what about mitzvot? Isn't God going to ask me why I ate that cheeseburger or why I went to the mall on Shabbat? Won't God be curious as to why I went to synagogue only on the High Holy

Days? Doesn't God care at all that I wear clothing made of linen and wool at the same time?!? All signs point to no. Rava is telling us that life is much more than the sum total of your deeds. One's life should be guided by principles, morals, and ethics, not simply acts that may carry no personal meaning. Could following mitzvot be a way to answer these questions in the affirmative? Yes. Is it the only way? No.

God cares about the way we act so that we in turn will care about the way we act. This teaching from Rava gives us a picture of a God that is more concerned with the big picture than the details.

So can you answer yes to all of these questions?

*According to Uri (and Rava), what kind of behavior does God **really** care about?*

Leah

According to the creation story in Genesis, human beings are created *b'tzelem Elohim*, in the image of God. The word *tzelem* is from the same Hebrew root word we would use to describe a photograph, a shadow, or a reflection in a mirror. This raises the question: If we are all created in God's image, how come we all look different? *B'tzelem Elohim* does not necessarily mean we look like God. No one knows what God looks like. It does mean that every single person we meet reflects God's image in some way.

I try to live my life by this principle. This is probably the biggest challenge of living Jewishly. It is one thing to say that we have to treat others with dignity and respect. It is a completely different thing to say that we have to treat people as if they were a reflection of the divine spirit.

Take a minute to walk through your day. How many people did you see, walk past, or talk to? How did each person reflect God's image? How did you treat each person? Did *you* reflect God's image to all the people you saw today? Pretty tough, isn't it?

Once in a while, when I am having trouble seeing the divine in the people around me, I try to take a minute to find one thing about each person that may be a reflection of God. I try saying to myself, "God must have a great sense of humor, since that student in my Hebrew school class is telling jokes and giggling with her best friend," or "God must think it's really important to fight for this cause, since my classmates keep asking me to give money and sign petitions and go to rallies," or "God must want me to spend time with my family, since my mom has called three times asking when I'm coming home for a visit."

According to Leah, how does being created B'Tzelem Elohim *help us to guide our actions?*

Commandments

It's your job to write ten—and only ten—rules about how people should behave. These are your ten commandments.

Before you begin writing rules, think about a few things. Should people follow these rules because God wants us to? (If that's the case, how do you pick ten rules? How do we know what God wants us to do?) Should these be rules that help people to get along, or should they be rules that help people be closer to God? Or both?

As you think about your list, you may want to consult with Justin, Uri, and Leah.

Chapter 12
Afterlife

Have you ever been to a funeral, or been talking to someone in mourning, and heard the phrase "He's in a better place now"?

The idea is that something happened to the person who died, and now he or she is—in some way—in a different place. Maybe it means that everyone who dies goes to some special place (Heaven? Valhalla?), and they all hang out together, having a grand ol' time. Maybe it means that the person's soul (whatever that means) is "at rest." Maybe we're not sure what it means, but people say it because it makes them feel better.

Imagine that you're having a conversation with someone who recently lost a loved one. The person says to you, "Where do you think (insert loved one's name) is?"

How would you answer?

As you ponder, ask yourself the following:

1. Is there a part of us—a soul, a spirit, an essence—that is more eternal than our bodies?

2. Is there any way that living people can know what happens to people after they die?

3. Why do you think this question matters so much to so many people?

We asked, "Where do people go when they die?"

Lisa

This is such a difficult question for anyone to answer. How can we be exactly sure where people go when they die? It is hard enough keeping track of people when they are alive; how are we supposed to know where they go when they die? When I was growing up my parents did not allow me to believe in the afterlife. My dad learned from his mother that when people die they are dead, and they stay in a wooden box in the ground. I don't know about you, but that was very hard to handle. As I started thinking about it and learning about how other religions and Judaism view death, I saw that part of what my dad said was true.

My belief is that when people are alive they give of themselves in a way that touches others around them that continues long after they have left this life. If you think very hard right now, can you hear your parents or grandparents saying something to you in your head? You might be able to hear "If you make that face any longer, it could stay that way." Those voices in your head of your loved ones are the pieces of them that stay with you. It is possible that when people die all of their words of wisdom and words of love stay with those around them, carrying on their life's work forever. We are all influenced by those around us, those words of wisdom that make us who we are. When people die their good deeds get dispersed into each person they have ever known.

According to Lisa, how do people who die manage to continue to be present in the lives of people around them?

88

Jennifer

In our daily morning blessings we recite *Elohai n'shama shenatata bi t'horah hi* (My God, the soul You have given me is pure). When we are born, God breathes life into our bodies, and that breath of God, that "Divine spark" that we each get, is the soul. It is the sacred, pure holiness within us that reaches Godward at all times, whether we notice it or acknowledge it at all. Throughout our lives our bodies act as physical vessels for that Divine spark, as casings to hold the breath of God inside, and as physical mechanisms that enable us to act as we need to in this world. When we die it is the physical body and organs that die, that cease to work in a manner necessary to sustain life. The soul, on the other hand, reconnects with its source; it goes back to God. It is like a candle flame that is about to go out. First the orange part of the flame, the outermost casing representing our physical bodies, becomes non-existent. The inner blue portion of the flame represents the outer soul, and inside it is a white spark of light, the last part of the candle flame to be extinguished. It does not so much "go out" as it ascends upwards in a line of smoke. It is like the soul being propelled toward a reunification with God by the Divine breath inside of it.

The soul, while being the "breath of God," is also our individual essence, who we truly are or who we were truly meant to be as people. I believe that when we die God recognizes the life journey and the spiritual journey that each soul has taken, and I would like to believe that those souls that did well in this world (those who looked out for others, those who lived up to their potential, those who were good people) are rewarded by being able to reside close to God (the Ultimate Source) and being nourished by God for eternity.

According to Jennifer, how are souls like flames?

Danya

The first person I saw die was my mother, when I was twenty years old. Many years later I worked as a chaplain in a hospital, in the wing that was nicknamed "the last stop before Heaven." It's a place for very, very sick people, and a lot of my patients died while I was with them. Every single time—with my mother, and then with the patients I served—I would experience strange things that are kind of hard to explain. There would be this tremendous tension in the room, the air would get very thick, very heavy, and as death crept closer it got more intense. And then it would be as though something started to glow, almost—this sense of mystery and power where everything is radiating in the slow place outside of time. And then, another moment later, the person would be gone, and the feeling in the air was as if a fever had broken—the tension was suddenly gone. Sometimes I'd know that someone had died from the feeling in the air instead of from the bleeps of the monitors they were plugged into.

I don't know what it means. I'll only know what really happens after we die after I've gone and done it myself—from this side of life, we're all just guessing. But over the years I've come to believe that dying is very safe. I think of a wave that sees the beach up ahead and starts to panic about crashing on sand—the end of life as it knows itself, the end of this form. And then suddenly the wave remembers with relief that it's been water the whole time. That there's only ever been water.

Jewish tradition says that the Divine presence hovers over the head of the dying, and that dying is the ultimate personal Yom Kippur—everything is atoned for; all we've done in this world is washed clean. It feels clear to me from my experiences that God is very close by as people die, perhaps closer than we can ever get during normal life. I don't believe that after we die that there's a hard stop, that everything just goes black. I also don't necessarily believe that we get to retain the personalities we had—though what do I know? I'm just another living person making a guess. I just know that when I think about death I think of waves rolling back from the shore, or an ice cube melting slowly in a glass of water. And I'm not afraid at all.

Why isn't Danya afraid of death?

Afterlife

You've been invited to give a talk to a group of high school students. The topic of the talk is "Different Attitudes on Afterlife." You'll be on a panel with other presenters who are all believers in different religions.

Your job is to explain your Jewish view on what happens after someone dies. You don't need to represent *all* Jews, just yourself.

Prepare a speech outline for a five-minute talk. What do you think happens to people after they die? How do your beliefs compare to traditional Jewish beliefs, or to what other religions believe? (It might help to do some research in a library or on the internet.)

As you prepare your notes you'll probably want to check back with Lisa, Jennifer, and Danya.

Chapter 13
Getting close to God

This book has been all about thinking about God. We've been thinking in abstract terms about abstract ideas. When people take philosophy classes or read books about theology, sometimes they complain about all the abstract stuff. They want God to be real.

This is the chapter where God gets real.

You can think about God and your beliefs all day long. But at some point you have to answer the question: So what?

How does God enter into your life? What kind of relationship do you have with God? Where, when, and how do you get close to God?

As you think about this big question, consider:

1. Have you ever felt close to God? If so, what was it about the experience that made it special?

2. Are there ways of getting close to God that really work for you? Are there ways that really don't work?

3. Where do you find God in your life?

We asked,
"How do I get close to God?"

Melissa

We each need to look deep within ourselves to identify what we need in order to connect to our Judaism. I have a friend who hikes to the tallest peaks to feel closer to God and another who through meditation can find God in her living room. Some people find God at the *Kotel* (the Wailing Wall) in Jerusalem, and there are others who relish the mosh pit at a youth-group singalong.

Our tradition offers many different accessories to help us connect to Judaism. Ritual accessories like *tefillin* and *tallit* have the power to bring us closer to the Divine. But they are no substitute for a *lev tahor* (a pure heart) and *kavanah* (intention). I preach the notion of choice through knowledge. How can we do something without understanding it? There is no choice without knowledge. First we must learn about the mitzvot associated with each item. We read in the *v'Ahavta* about binding the word of God on our head and arm: Is that *tefillin*? The prayer, an excerpt from the book of Exodus, also explains the fringes we are commanded to wear on our four-cornered garments; does this mean wearing a *tallit katan* (a tiny prayer shawl) under our clothes at all times or wearing an artistic *tallit* during morning prayers? Being told to cover our head could mean a *kippah*, a baseball cap, or a *kefiyah*.

And for young women, all of these accessories are understood in traditional circles as appling only to men. So how are we to understand our connection to these items? Should we embrace what was considered male to achieve gender equality or create our own traditions that are unique for women? Different communities have different norms, but what do you want to do?

Once you know, make the choice. Find your way to connect with God.

How does choosing through knowledge help Melissa get closer to God?

Jennifer

The best example that I have come across of my belief about how one gets close to God comes from Buddhist meditation teacher Jack Kornfield, who wrote: "To meditate and pray and listen is like throwing the doors and windows open. You can't plan for the breeze." God is constantly present around us, but we are not always aware of it. If we seek to draw near to God, however, we must always be ready to feel God's presence; we must always be open to encountering the Divine in our lives.

Thousands of years ago, when the Temple in Israel was standing and animal sacrifices were being offered upon its altars, the Temple was seen as the "house of God"; it was where God stayed when He was in Jerusalem. The priests, however, believed that God went in and out of the Temple (God was, then, not always at home). To make God comfortable when He was at home, and to entice Him to stay a while, the priests would offer the sacrifices that they believed God liked most. They did this every day, whether or not they believed God was actually in or near the Temple. It was an act of perpetual readiness, work that was performed *just in case* God happened to show up. The priests, for the most part, never knew when God would come back home, so they kept the sacrifices and offerings burning so that when God did come, they would be ready for Him.

We can learn a lot from the Temple priests. Being close to God is not necessarily about doing anything differently physically from day to day; rather, it is about learning how to be open and ready to experience God's presence when we are somehow fortunate enough to have the opportunity. There are, of course, ways and methods to increase one's chances. Jewish rituals and practices are full of meaningful actions that we can take in an attempt to draw closer to God. Some may work immediately, and some, we may find, do not work for us at all. Coming close to God, though, is about struggling and wrestling with all of these issues and questions. God is found when we live up to our potential as "Israel" (as wrestlers with God), and God is found as we make our way on our spiritual and religious journeys.

According to Jennifer, what does it mean to be "ready" for God?

Leah

There are many paths toward God, and you have to find your own.

Jews throughout history tried many ways of moving towards God. In the Bible people devised a system of sacrificing animals in the Temple as their way of connecting with God. When the Temple was destroyed, the rabbis who wrote the Talmud decided that they would use prayer and mitzvot as a way of getting close to God. This system still works for a lot of people. But it's always good to try something different.

Nachman of Bratslav would go out into the woods and meditate among all the living things in his world. There he felt he could actually talk to God.

Isaac Luria thought that the world was broken and that we could come closer to God by trying to put the pieces back together. This is where the idea of *tikkun olam* came from. Today many Jewish people use that phrase to refer to social action. By making the world a better place we can move closer to God.

Abraham Joshua Heschel would say that through prayer we invite God to be a part of our lives by the "opening of a window to Him in our will".

Martin Buber talks about the ideal relationship with God, or with another person, as an "I–Thou" relationship. This is a relationship in which two people, or one person and God, form a connection in which they are completely equal and completely focused on each other.

I've always felt—sort of in line with what Buber said—that we come close to God by getting close to other human beings. Because we are all created in the image of God, knowing people is really the closest thing we have to knowing God. Today's technology allows us to communicate with people all over the world, but often we barely notice the person next to us. When two people interact with each other in a way that is loving and respectful, open and trusting, I think they are interacting with God as well.

I like to think of our closeness to God as two people standing on opposite sides of a door. We may choose to move closer to or farther away from God, but God is always right on the other side. The big question is, are we going to open the door?

According to Leah, what can we learn about closeness to God from Nachman of Bratslav, Isaac Luria, A.J. Heschel, and Martin Buber?

Rachel K.

Every Friday night I give my daughter the traditional priestly blessing at the Shabbat table. I say, "May God bless you and keep you. May God shine God's face on you and be gracious to you. May God turn with favor toward you and grant you peace." "May God shine God's face on you"—what on earth could this mean? How can a faceless God shine a face on us? I have come to realize that the Divine face shines on us by allowing us to shine our face on others. Each time we look into another person's eyes and spend time really listening to what she has to say, we are allowing God to shine upon us. It is through these interactions that we come to know the voice of compassion, truth, and holiness. It is through these interactions that we come to know God.

According to Rachel K., how does God's face "shine" on us?

Getting Close

At the end of every chapter, this book has given you an assignment that asks you to think about the chapter's theological
question.

This chapter is a bit different. There's no hypothetical question or
creative art project.

Here's your assignment: Try to get close to God. That's all. Do
whatever it is you do that helps you get close to God. If you're
not sure what to do, or if you're not sure if you believe in God,
try some of the ways that Melissa, Jennifer, Leah, and Rachel K.
suggest.

Journal about your experiences and share them with a friend.

Author Bios

Shira

Shira Batalion was trained as a cantor at the Reconstructionist Rabbinical College in Philadelphia. She now works as the education director of Congregation Bet Haverim, a progressive Reconstructionist synagogue founded by the gay and lesbian community in Atlanta, GA. Prior to grad school she lived in West Africa, traveled cross-country, worked in prisons, taught juvenile weapons offenders, and managed an organic garden. Today Shira uses Jewish values and the power of prayer and song to learn and teach how to live in healthy communities and recognize our interdependence across cultures so we may together create a peaceful and sustainable world.

Rachel B.

Rachel Barenblat is a student in the Aleph rabbinic program. She is an active member of and rabbinic intern at Congregation Beth Israel in North Adams, MA. She writes regularly about Judaism at her blog, *Velveteen Rabbi*, and has contributed to *Essential Torah* (Schocken, 2006) and *The Women's Seder Source Book* (Jewish Lights, 2003). She is the creator of the *Velveteen Rabbi's Haggadah for Pesach*, a homegrown haggadah used around the world. She holds an MFA in writing and literature from Bennington and is author of three collections of poetry, most recently *chaplainbook* (laupe house, 2006). She lives in western Massachusetts with her husband Ethan Zuckerman.

Lydia

Lydia Bloom is a rabbinic student at HUC-JIR in Los Angeles. During her summers she has worked for Henry S. Jacobs Camp, most recently as the education director. Before beginning her journey as a rabbinic student Lydia served full-time as the educator for Congregation Beth Israel in Jackson, Mississippi, and directed and implemented adult and youth educational programming. Prior to this Lydia received her undergraduate degree from the University of Texas at Austin, where she majored in

Honors Humanities and Middle Eastern Studies. Lydia has also spent time exploring various countries such as Peru and South Africa, as well as participating in a rabbinic delegation to El Salvador with the American Jewish World Service. She recently married Dan Medwin, also a rabbinic student.

Dan

Dan Medwin is working toward being ordained as a Reform rabbi from HUC-JIR with a master's in Jewish education by 2010. He is married to Lydia, his best friend and classmate, whom he met in Israel during their first year of rabbinical school. Also, to the best of his knowledge, he will be a part of the first mother–son rabbinic family in the U.S. (and the second in all of history). Dan's undergraduate degree is in sociology and Near Eastern & Judaic studies from Brandeis University. Dan grew up in Wilmington, Delaware. He enjoys spending time outdoors, camping and hiking, and playing with any gadgets he can find.

Justin

Justin Goldstein is a student at the Ziegler School of Rabbinic Studies in Los Angeles, CA. Growing up secular, Justin forged his Jewish identity when he asked his parents to join a congregation in order that he become a bar mitzvah. Since then Jewishness has driven Justin's life. Justin hopes to bring to the rabbinate a love of Torah and the pursuit of justice for all peoples. The impetus that guides Justin's desire for the rabbinate is an understanding that if assimilation is the biggest threat the Jewish people face today, education is our greatest weapon against that threat.

Melissa

Melissa Simon is a rabbinical and Jewish education student at HUC-JIR in New York and also attended HUC-JIR in Cincinnati. She is the children's educator at Congregation Beth Simchat Torah in New York City and has served in pulpits at Temple Beth Sholom in Ishpeming, Michigan, and at Denison University in Granville, Ohio. Melissa worked on summer social justice programs for high school students, including NFTY Bay Area Mitzvah Corps and PANIM Summer JAM. She has lived all over the world, from Boston to Beijing, from San Francisco to South Hadley, Massachusetts, and most recently spent a year studying in Jerusalem. A 2004 graduate of Mount Holyoke College, Melissa is a passionate advocate for social justice, particularly concerning Israel, AIDS education, gay rights, and women's rights.

Joel S.

Joel Shickman is currently the Rosh Musica at Camp Ramah in California and is pursuing his Smicha at the Ziegler School of Rabbinic Studies. He lives in Southern California with his wife and three boys, who all try to keep him busy and honest.

Ari

Ari Margolis is a rabbinical student at HUC-JIR in Los Angeles. He grew up in a Reform congregation in Hollywood, FL. Abandoning his Jewish journey for a while, he pursued a career in chemical engineering, earning a B.S. from Northwestern University while working in semiconductor research. This process allowed him to discover that his scientific work was strengthening his religious ideology and diminishing his human interaction, leading him eventually to the rabbinate, where he will be able to work on bridging the gaps between science and faith while also bringing together individuals within a congregation.

Danya

Danya Ruttenberg is the editor of *Yentl's Revenge: The Next Wave of Jewish Feminism* (Seal Press), author of *Surprised By God: How I Learned to Stop Worrying and Love Religion* (forthcoming from Beacon Press), and editor of *Sex and Judaism* (forthcoming from NYU Press). She will be ordained as a rabbi by the American Jewish University in Los Angeles in May, 2008. Danya has been published in a wide variety of books and periodicals, from *Encyclopedia Judaica* and the *Best Jewish Writing* series to *Bitchfest* and *The Women's Movement Today: An*

Encyclopedia of Third-Wave Feminism. Danya has had the great privilege to work with Jewish teenagers in a number of different settings, and they always manage to kick her butt (in a good way).

Isaac

Isaac Saposnik is a student at the Reconstructionist Rabbinical College. He is the director of No'ar Hadash: The Reconstructionist Youth Movement and assistant director of Camp JRF. A graduate of Tufts University, Isaac has taught at synagogues, camps, youth events, and professional development conferences across the country. A product of Jewish summer camps and youth groups, Isaac spent more than a decade as a camper and staff member at Olin-Sang-Ruby Union Institute and served as regional advisor for the NFTY Chicago Area and Northern Regions, for which he was a recipient of the first NFTY President's Award.

Leah

Leah Rachel Berkowitz is a rabbinic and education student at HUC-JIR in New York. She grew up in Broomall, and graduated from Brandeis University. Leah has served in congregations and camps, hospitals and Hillels all over the Eastern seaboard. Everything she knows about God—her faith and her questions—she learned from her family, her friends, and the communities she has found at Temple Sholom in Broomall, URJ Camp Harlam, NFTY, Brandeis University Reform Chavurah, and HUC-JIR.

Uri

Uri Allen teaches Jewish studies at the New Community Jewish High School in Los Angeles. In addition to teaching, Uri coaches girls' and boys' volleyball and is the *tefillah* coordinator for the school. In his spare time Uri is a founding *gabbai* of PicoEgal, a new *davening* community in the Pico/Robertson neighborhood in LA.

Sara

Sara Mason is studying to be a rabbi and an educator at HUC-JIR in Los Angeles. She's a graduate of Brandeis University and the DeLeT program and has served in student pulpits in Lancaster, CA, and UCLA Hillel. She's also worked at URJ Camp Newman, the Rashi School (Newton, MA), Temple Isaiah (Beverly Hills, CA), Temple Beth Shalom (Santa Ana, CA), and Congregation Or Ami (Calabasas, CA). Her favorite Beatle is Ringo.

Rachel K.

Rachel Kobrin is a rabbinical student at the Ziegler School of Rabbinic Studies at the American Jewish University. She is deeply committed to fostering spiritual communities that engage and inspire 21st-century American Jews. Rachel has shared her passion for Jewish life with children, teens, and adults at synagogues, camps, and Hillels throughout the country. Thanks to their three-year-old daughter Noa, Rachel and her husband Rick are reminded daily of the mysterious and wondrous nature of God.

Jennifer

Jennifer Frenkel is a rabbinical student at HUC-JIR in Cincinnati. She is originally from Oak Park, Michigan, and graduated from Michigan State University with a Bachelor of Arts degree in anthropology and a specialization in Jewish studies. Jennifer has served as the student rabbi of Temple B'nai Israel in Petoskey, Michigan, and Congregation Beth El in Saginaw, Michigan. She has also served as the rabbinic intern at the Isaac M. Wise Temple in Cincinnati, Ohio. She has worked in religious and Hebrew school classrooms for over nine years and is also a chaplain intern at The Jewish Hospital in Cincinnati.

Josh L.

Joshua Seth Ladon lives in Jerusalem, Israel, where he is a student of Jewish philosophy at the Tel Aviv University as well as the Melamdim School for Teacher Training at the Shalom Hartman Institute. He grew up in Worcester, MA, and moved to Denver, CO, before high school. He is a graduate of Washington University in St. Louis and after college learned at the Conservative Yeshiva for two years.

Sadie

Sadie Reuben is a rabbinical student at HUC-JIR in Los Angeles. From childhood Sadie was very involved and devoted to her Jewish community. She went to the Phoenix Hebrew Academy, was a leader in NFTY-Southwest, and was involved in Hillel at the University of Arizona. Born and raised in Phoenix, Arizona, Sadie now lives in Los Angeles. She has worked in student pulpits at Kelowna, British Columbia, and UCLA Hillel.

Lisa

Lisa Delson is a rabbinical student at HUC-JIR in Cincinnati and looking forward to ordination in 2009. She is originally from Columbus, Ohio, and participated in NFTY throughout her high school years. Prior to rabbinical school Lisa graduated from the University of Cincinnati with a B.A. in sociology. Lisa is passionate about Jewish youth education and social justice issues. When she is not studying or preparing to be a rabbi, she can be found playing a round of golf with her friends and family.

Josh B.

Josh Barkin, the editor, is a recent graduate of HUC-JIR in Los Angeles, where he received master's degrees in Jewish education and Jewish communal service. As an undergrad he was one of the only Jews at Ripon College in Ripon, Wisconsin, where he double-majored in politics and religion. Josh has been a page designer and sports reporter for the Oshkosh Northwestern (Oshkosh, WI) and worked at the World Union of Progressive Judaism in Jerusalem, the Bureau of Jewish Education of Greater Los Angeles, and at lots of congregational schools. Now he works at Torah Aura Productions. He felt closest to God during the final moments of Game 1 of the 1988 World Series.